Familiars, Thought Forms & Energy Balls Creating Magic Entities

By
E.M. Fairchilde

Familiars, Thought Forms & Energy Balls
Creating Magic Entities

Interior design by E.M. Fairchilde

Cover photo: www.depositphotos.com
Interior photos from depositphotos.com and my own collection
Printed in the United States of America

About the Author

I have a Bachelor of Science degree in Psychology, but the darker side of the science appealed to me more. Paranormal psychology fascinates me to this day. Metaphysical theories have interested me most of my life and led me to begin studying and using Wiccan concepts several years ago. I consider myself an eclectic, solitary, even chaotic witch, and live with my family, my cat Lola, and one very stubborn Basset Hound named Fritz.

Contact

emfairchilde@gmail.com

I dedicate this collection to beginner witches everywhere!

The Magic Is Within You

Books by E. M. Fairchilde

Book of Shadows, Beginner's Guide, Information & Workbook
Moon Phase Rituals Made Easy, Beginner's Guide & Workbook
Sabats and Esbats, Beginner's Guide
Banishing, Binding, Cursing, & Hexing, Beginner's Guide
What Kind of Witch are You?
Centering, Grounding & Shielding, Beginner's Guide
The Elements, Beginner's Guide
The Colors of Magic…White, Black & Gray
Sigils & Chaos Magic, Beginner's Guide
Goddess Magic & Energy, Beginner's Guide
Energize your Magic using Candles, Herbs, Oils & Stones, Beginner's Guide
The Beginner Witch's Collection Book One
The Beginner Witch's Collection Book Two
Covens, Circles, Groups & Gatherings, Beginner's Guide
The Beginner Witch's Collection Book Three
Altars, Circles & Sacred Spaces, Beginner's Guide
Spells, Incantations, Invocations, Evocations & Rituals, Beginner's Guide
Calling the Quarters, Beginner's Guide
Talismans, Amulets, Lucky Charms & Symbols, Beginner's Guide
The Beginner Witch's Collection Book Four

Poppets, Voodoo Dolls and Effigies
Creating Magic Entities:
Familiars, Thought Forms & Energy Balls

Beginner Books Coming Soon
Cleansing, Charging & Consecrating
5 Tenets of Magic:
Concentration, Regularity, Intent, Focus, & Purpose
The Beginner Witch's Collection, Book Five

Fiction
Book One of the NEK Series, Unintentional Magic
Book Two of the NEK Series, TBA
The Coven in the North Woods Series
The Water Street Witch
The Witch Next Door

Disclaimer

The methods described in this book are my personal thoughts and experiences. I realize others may practice the craft differently, and so, may use different methods. My methods are not intended to be a definitive set of instructions for using the craft. You may discover other methods and materials to carry out and achieve the same results. The craft is all about personal power, and using that special power to achieve, and manifest your life goals.

This book is not a life manual. The contents are not intended to offend. If you do not believe in the paranormal, then this book is not for you.

Forward

If you're reading this book, more than likely, you are interested in magic, the Wiccan way, and are beginning your journey. My hope is that the information provided will help. I believe, as I state throughout this book, practicing magic is not complicated, it is an elemental down to earth, way of life. In a sense, we all use magic daily; we're just not aware of it. We become aware of our power when we *actively* pursue the ins and outs of making things happen intentionally.

So, for those of you who are interested in learning some of the many facets of Paganism, Wicca, or Witchcraft and want to try something different, welcome to my magical world! Use this book as general knowledge as you begin your journey.

I believe using magic should be simple. Don't get bogged down with the words used to define the process. They only feel intimidating to you now because they are not part of your current daily vocabulary. Once you know the basics of magic, and the definitions of words that will come up often in your quest for knowledge about magic, you'll be comfortable. I hope my simplified approach will help you, and if you want to learn a few things about the craft, feel free to use the information provided in this ***beginner's guide*** for a thought-provoking journey.

Harm and Consequences

Everything we do in life has consequences. If you are not already practicing, weigh the consequences you think will occur as you journey through magic. And if practicing the craft will benefit you in an effective way then go ahead and begin.

'Do no harm, harm no one, no harm be done' is an interesting concept. And it is an excellent concept to follow. But harm is a vague word and an even more nebulous idea. If I harm someone who has done harm to me, is this a bad idea? If a killer is harmed while being pursued, is pursuing him a bad idea? You will have to decide for yourself what harm means to you and then live with your decisions as to how you use it.

Consequence is another interesting word and an even more interesting concept. Consequences can be positive or negative. But, sometimes, until all is said and done with certain actions, it is hard to know if the outcomes have been positive or negative, and therefore the consequences of these outcomes, because there is always some sort of consequence.

Using magic opens the door to many would-be consequences so be sure you can live with the outcome of your work. Magic is like anything, how you use it is what determines its good or bad label. A knife can be good or bad, it depends on what you do with it. Magic is the same. It's an energy that you manipulate.

Practicing as a solitary witch leaves it entirely up to you the kinds of magic you work with. Some individuals, covens and groups frown on manipulative magic. You will have to decide for yourself your comfort level with the many facets of magic. If something doesn't resonate with you, don't do it, because the outcome may not be what you were expecting. On the other hand, if you are open to all or most kinds of magic because you are trying to find what *will* work for you, then use it. But, use it wisely.

One thing to consider when trying out new magical practices is the *way* you carry out your practice determines your outcome. For example, just as some types of magic may be more manipulative than others, so might lighter magic if you are using it in a manipulative manner.

If you create your own spells and magic tools, you will know precisely how and what they are used for and what they mean because you are the creator and your intentions are clear. However, if you purchase spells or tools, make sure you know what they mean, and how to use them because some spells and tools may have negative connotations based solely on the person's thought process who created them. This would come apparent to you if the spell or tools you purchased were supposed to render a positive result, but the opposite occurred.

Always cleanse anything new you've found or purchased whether it is for use with your practice or not because you have no idea how many hands and energies it had passed through before it became yours. You certainly don't want bad energy to permeate around and through you because it may hinder your life, livelihood, home, and practice. There are many simple cleansing tools and spells that don't involve an extensive ritual. Just like shielding, your shield can be as simple as saying, "shields up." Your cleansing can be just as simple. Find what works for you.

Energy

Energy is an interesting concept. Everything revolves around energy. When I worked for corporate America, I used to have a saying, "You put your energy into a project, and it works, you take your energy out of the project and it falls apart." And that was always true for me. But if that's true, then why is it that some people can accomplish what others can't? I believe it circles back to energy. If you are attempting something that is not for you, it won't work no matter what you put into it; in fact, you may just be wasting good energy that might be better used elsewhere.

All magic is manipulative because we use tools and energies to perform rituals for an outcome. Energy is neither good nor bad, just as manipulating energy is neither good nor bad, again it depends on how we manipulate it. For example, I can use my fire bowl as part of a ritual I am performing by burning a paper on which I've written something I wish to banish from my life. In this case, the fire (energy) is contained, and when the paper is burned, the fire goes out. But that same fire (energy) can also be destructive when it is not watched and gets out of control. So, we can say that energy can be constructive and or destructive. But even that is a vague statement because the fire we are using to burn the paper is destructive in that it destroys the paper. The only difference is that we control one fire. We manipulate the fire to do our will.

When it comes to magic, it is all about how we use energy, how we control it, how we move it around to accomplish what we set out to accomplish. So, when it comes to what some call manipulative magic, yes, it is manipulative, but it depends on how we manipulate it that makes it good or bad.

I know a person who doesn't practice the craft. At least she doesn't practice it consciously. Yet, whenever she really wants something, she energizes herself to such a high frequency that she obtains what she wants almost immediately. She says she focuses on only what she wants and nothing else, and she manifests. Her energy is high. I've seen her do this repeatedly. But, here's the crux, because she doesn't think through what she's going after, in other words, she doesn't have a plan, a lot of the time she has wasted her energy because what she has gotten turns out not to be what she thought it was to begin with. She goes through an equal

amount of energy getting rid of what she set out to get.
An interesting thing about energy where Covens, Circles, Gatherings, and Groups are concerned—We are energy. Each of us is surrounded by an energy field and we emit that energy.

Have you ever been in someone's presence and felt their bad energy? Or someone walks into a room full of people and suddenly the atmosphere changes. You feel drained. You feel as if the life force has been sucked out of you. Or you get nervous, almost scared. You may feel a sense of dread as if something bad is about to happen. We've all experienced this around certain people. Their energy is negative, problematic.

By the same token you can be in a room full of boring people wondering how you're going to make it through the meeting, or whatever the function is, and suddenly someone comes into the room and your spirits are lifted, you feel as if you could soar. Your entire demeanor changes and the mood of energy of the room lifts and explodes with possibilities. We've all felt that energy as well.

In ***a coven, circle, gathering, or group,*** you will run into several kinds of energy. The more people who are gathered together the more likely there is going to be a mixture of energy. But what if there is more negative energy? How does a gathering raise the energy level high enough to accomplish a task if they are bogged down by bad energy? There is an old saying that one rotten apple can spoil the bushel. If so, how do groups function with this kind of rotten apple energy?

There is a woman in my town who practices the craft. She is out of the broom closet, so everyone knows she is a witch. She is a member of a large ***circle*** that gets together for moon phases, Sabats, and Esbats. But here's the thing—this woman is surrounded by and emits negative energy. I've run into her in town, and I stay clear! She posts on her social media page constantly, as in several times a day. Her posts are all woe is me. She's depressed, she can't even get out of her recliner to do the laundry or go shopping, her life is full of pain and strife. Nobody understands her, not her husband, friends, or children. The tales of woe go on and on and on! She is without a doubt the most negative person I have ever come across! I got exhausted just reading her posts, so I put her on hide. My point here is, if this woman is part of a circle, what kind of energy does she bring with her? And if there are more than one like her in the circle and ***one*** bad apple spoils the bushel, how do they ever accomplish anything?

This is why I prefer to do my magic as a solitary. I know my own energy and I know when to use it and when not to. I can control my energy. And I believe in order to accomplish anything you are attempting to do using magic, you have to elevate the energy, and to me, that means one focal point. In a group I question how that can happen.

My own energy is scattered, and I must work hard to reign it in so I can use it for my magic. One reason I love practicing the craft is it forces me to focus on what I'm doing with my energy. I've used metaphysical concepts most of my life, so turning to the craft was easy. In a lot of ways, it's all remarkably similar. It's all about focused energy and how you manipulate that energy. So, reign in your energy, and focus, focus, focus! You *are* the creator!

Ceremonies and Mood

I love ceremonies, and for me, a ceremony is created by setting a mood. I create a mood for almost everything I do. My mood enhancers are usually music and smell. I play smooth jazz, barely discernible when writing. If I am creating artistically, I play early rock and for rituals such as cleansing, charging, and consecrating, I play low, scarcely perceptible background sounds such as babbling brooks, wind, ocean waves, and birds.

I find my work more natural, more desirable, and more successful if I create an atmosphere. For sleep, I fill muslin bags with Lavender, Bay Leaf, Rosemary, and even Sage to slip in my pillowcase.

My morning ceremony for stretching is facing the north and stretching and saying, "Guide me today northern energy," facing the east, stretching and saying, "Guide me today eastern energy," facing the south, and stretching and saying, "Guide me today southern energy, and finally facing the west and stretching, and saying, "Guide me today western energy." This is a ceremony with a little bit of magic and some healthy stretching thrown in.

I burn candles and incense throughout the day because I love the smell, and I believe the fragrance keeps me and my home in a constant state of protection.

Does creating a mood and atmosphere take more time? Yes, but there are no short cuts if you desire success, and this is what works for me.
Focus on your intent, focus keenly on what it is you want to accomplish for your spell, ritual, or ceremony. Visualize it working for you, your home, your workplace, or another person. Rid your mind of all unwanted or negative energies. See and feel the adverse and negative energy leave. Speak your incantation with conviction, strength, and force of will in the perfect atmosphere you've created. The comfort and pleasure of your atmosphere, the endurance of your will, and the strength of your voice will bring forth your desired effect.

The ceremonies I use, I consider prep work for my magic. My ceremonies are nontraditional and fit my needs and comfort for practicing my kind of magic. But you are certainly welcome to use any of them if you feel the need to prep for your ceremonies. Since there is not a dogmatic approach to eclectic, solitary, chaos magic, you should perform it; however, you wish. Do what works for you!

Contents

Introduction

This is a beginner's guide written in simple terms to make it easy for you to harness and practice using your personal power to achieve personal goals. Sometimes we complicate things and make them more difficult than need be, and this causes confusion, so this book is written using simple, and basic terms. The key to using your personal power is focus, repetition, and intent. Keep it simple and focus, don't get overwhelmed or bogged down with terminologies. And practice your craft.

Learning how the various kinds of magic work in divination ensures consistency of the practice. The more you use and apply the basics, the more accomplished you will become. And you will feel competent and secure in using your personal power to achieve your goals. As you achieve your basic goals, your magic will advance to new levels.

All of this is simple when you break it down. With all witchcraft practices, remember the most basic rule, **'do no harm, harm no one,**

`no harm be done.' You are responsible for what you send out to the universe.

Your spells begin when you start forming a thought in your mind about your intention. The casting begins at that moment. Ensure your intentions, gather your tools, cleanse your work area, focus your mind, and then begin your work!

Magic Entities

Magic entities are formed and shaped in the mind of the creator. Like spells which begin with a thought, so do magic entities. The process of magic is all about thought, intention, energy, and creation. Our thoughts become intentions fed by energy which then come into being. So, in essence, magic entities are a mass of energy which we then form into a specific being that we send out to do our will.

Magic entities are generally formed with a specific purpose in mind. Each magical entity you create is an individual and will have individual attributes. For example, you may create an entity to find healing, love, prosperity, or success. You may be more specific and create your magical entity to gather information for a new job, a new home, even a new area where you may want to live. Magical entities may be short-or long-term energy masses. If you use one for a short-term project, when the project is complete, you will call the entity home, thank it, and release it back to where it began. You, as the creating force are in control of the magic entity you create.

It is most important to remember that it is ***your*** energy that is used to move the magic entity in the direction you have chosen. You must be clear as to your intention for the magic entity or you will end up with a mass of swirling confused energy about you that has no direction and may create havoc. Magic entities must have a purpose, rules, some sort of time frame in which to create the desired effect, and a means of termination so the energy is not left floating about when the original purpose has been satisfied. The easiest way to terminate the magic entity is to thank it for the work it did, and then mentally say goodbye.

Using magical entities as a part of your magic practice can bring about desired outcomes. For example, a magical entity has a specific purpose so when you use the entity you are not leaving it up to the universe to decide which way your desire will come about. The magical entity goes directly to the source of your desired outcome and weaves its energy around the source in order to deliver your desire back to you.

Magic entities are a part of the person who creates them, they are an extension of their creator. The entity gains its energy through the work of the creator.

Magic in any form is best when it is practiced consistently. To gain and keep control of energy, practitioners of magic must work with and recognize energy in all its forms. Once we do this, we are able to control energy and once we are able to control energy, we have mastered magic and our power grows.

Steps for creating Magic Entities—

State your desire in writing

Type of entity you may need in writing

Define your goals

Pros and cons regarding your desire in writing

Narrowing down the pros and cons in writing

Accepting pros and cons, keep what you need, discard the rest

Purpose for the entity in writing

Tasks for the entity in writing

Perform a cleansing and consecrating ritual

Create the entity

Name the entity-define appearance

Rules for the entity

Goals for the entity

Timeframe for achievement of goals

Releasing the entity after goals are achieved

Creating magic entities is not something you want to do lightly because the entity is a part of you, created as an extension of you. The magic entity is your energy made manifest in form. This type of magic can be used as white, gray, or black magic. You decide what and how the entity will work for you. I work with general purpose entities. They are *on call* as needed. My general-purpose entities are health, wealth, success, happiness, and love.

Generally speaking, magical entities are familiars, thought forms, and energy balls. It is important to note here that a familiar may also manifest as more than an energy force.

Familiars

A familiar is usually an animal companion. A familiar is a helper, a servant used in spell work or magic. It is generally in the form of an animal. Familiars are bonded to the person they serve, but they tend to have their own personalities. Animals who appear in our lives unexpectedly may well be Familiars, such as a stray cat showing up on your doorstep. Generally, an animal Familiar will select you, you do not select the Familiar. But you may certainly summon or seek a Familiar by doing a spell that invites one to join you and become a part of your life.

According to folklore, Familiars were sent out to gather information and spy. They were and are also used for protection. Familiars are generally real live animals such as rabbits, dogs and cats, rodents, birds such as ravens or owls, or even reptiles. But they can also be with you in spirit, or artistically created. Familiars are thought of as a servant and companion to the practitioner and usually have magical powers.

Key words associated with Familiars—

Domestic animal
Wild animal
Rodent
Reptile
Magical
Powerful

Ceremonies and rituals—When a Familiar approaches you, for example shows up on your doorstep, you must not assume it is your Familiar. You should do a ceremony where you meditate, pass your hands over the animal, and ask it if it is or desires to be your Familiar. You will receive some sort of sign if the animal is indeed your Familiar.

Spells or incantations to summon a Familiar—

By the morning sun that shines,
And the moon that glows at night,
I summon you to bring to me
A Familiar who is right.
A bark, a tweet, a croak, a mew,
That I may know it's true.
Hear me now, hear my plea,
And join me with
The one who's meant to be.
Blessed be.

Notes: Use these pages to write your own spells, rituals, or ideas.

Thoughtforms

Thoughtforms are bundles of psychic energy created by a magic practitioner to work for them. Thoughtforms are not physical entities. Thoughtforms can be used for many different purposes. When creating Thoughtforms you should have a purpose in mind as to what you want to achieve with this psychic energy. Weakly thought out Thoughtforms will not be effective. Powerful Thoughtforms must be precise and controlled. When you think about the idea of a Thoughtform, go back to a place where you have been in the company of a person whose negative or positive energy field was obvious to you. You actually felt their energy. Now imagine that energy sent out to work for that person. Energy is real, it isn't always seen but it is real. Thoughtforms are energy.

To create your own Thoughtform, there are several steps you should follow:

Have a goal in mind before you begin. What is it you want this Thoughtform to do?

Sit or lie down in a quiet room with nothing to disturb you.

Meditate, clear your mind of everything in the outside world.

Visualize light coming into you. The color of the light should correspond to the Thoughtform you are creating. For example, love is pink, red is lust or love, protection is yellow, money, abundance and success are green, power is purple, orange for overcoming blocks or hard times, blue is for healing, purple is for intuition, white is purity, cleansing, and black is generally used for binding, banishing, cursing, or hexing.

When you feel the energy start to rise in you, connect that energy to what it is you want the Thoughtform to do for you, and woosh that energy into the Thoughtform.

Briefly, very briefly say what it is you desire, and then push the Thoughtform out into the world to do your bidding. For example, you might say "bring me success at my job."

When the job is complete, call the Thoughtform back to you, and thank it, and release it back to nothing by saying something like, “your job is done, so it is.”

And, you can have several Thoughtforms out there doing your bidding, just make sure you keep track of the Thoughtforms you’ve sent out because if you fail to call them back when their jobs are finished, they will gather energy from other entities and could become out of control.

Key words associated with Thought Forms—

Energy
Emotion
Will
Desire
Projection

Ceremonies and rituals—The ceremony or ritual for a Thoughtform is twofold, it is in the creation listed in the steps above, and the dissolution when the Thoughtform has completed the task.

Spells or incantations when using your Thought Forms for spell work—In the incantation below, I used the word, Thoughtform. However, if you have named your Thoughtform, by all means use the name.

This is just a short incantation sent out to bring back success for a business. Success may be increased sales, which increases revenue, or it could be for increased community notoriety which might in turn increase the profit margin. You could change the word *business* to anything you might desire. And, where I used Thoughtform, if you have given it a name, by all means use the name instead.

I send this Thoughtform on its way,
To do my bidding, now, today.
Bring success for my business,
Bring it fast I say.
Go, now, be on your way!

Notes: Use these pages to write your own spells, rituals, or ideas.

Energy Balls

An Energy Ball is a ball of energy formed by you and sent out to the universe to do your bidding. Begin the process of creation by breathing in slowly through your nose, hold the breath for a few seconds, then expel the air through your lips. Do this until you feel a sense of peace.

To create an Energy Ball, you must focus and direct your energy into the ball. The easiest way to do this is through your hands. Begin by clapping your hands together several times to get the process started. Rubbing your hands together until you feel energy forming or clasping your hands together tightly until you feel energy is the second step. Do not stop either rubbing your palms or clasping your hands until you feel the energy rising through your body and into your hands. Concentrate on feeling the energy with a clear mind as you do this with your hands.

When you feel the energy, stop rubbing or clasping your hands and part them slightly. Your hands may feel warm, cold, or they may even vibrate. Let the energy flow and form it into a ball. Form this ball the same way you would if you were working with clay. As you are forming the ball, think about what you want this ball to do. When you feel the ball is ready, send it out to do your bidding. Deciding what you want the Energy Ball to do involves using the color process, for example, love is pink, red is lust or love, protection is yellow, money, abundance and success are green, power is purple, orange for overcoming blocks or hard times, blue is for healing, purple is for intuition, white is purity, cleansing, and black is generally used for binding, banishing, cursing, or hexing.

Energy Balls are fairly quick and easy to create. They are not time consuming like Thoughtforms, but they are equally as effective. Like Thoughtforms though, you need to dissipate the Energy Ball when the job is complete.

Key words associated with Energy Balls—

Focus
Concentration
Energy Direction

Ceremonies and rituals—The ceremony is in the creation as defined above. But, if you want to do a ritual as you create, you certainly may do so. Like most rituals you'd start by going to your sacred space, cleansing that space, drawing your circle, and then calling on any force you think you need.

Spells or incantations when using your Energy Balls for spell work—An incantation may go like this:

I send the yellow ball
Along the way.
To protect my ___________
Come what may.
Go now, do your thing
Take care of my loved one
Today.

Notes: Use these pages to write your own spells, rituals, or ideas.

Care and Caution

Like any type of magic, creating and working with entities comes with its own set of precautions. Working with entities tends towards the gray and black magic because you are not asking for or receiving permission from another when you direct the entity. So, you should be aware that your actions may have consequences. Even when we 'think' we are doing something beneficial for someone, that may not be the case. For example, you may think your sibling would be better off living in a different neighborhood, so you create a Thoughtform that causes havoc for your sibling where he currently lives. Your sibling is then forced to find a new place to live, but because he doesn't qualify for the neighborhood you think is desirable he actually ends up having to move to a neighborhood that is less desirable than where he was living before you sent out the Thoughtform. In this case, your sibling loses. So, you should plan carefully when you are sending out magic entities.

If you follow the Rede, or believe in karmic law, or 'do unto others', working with entities may not be your thing, or at least be careful how you use your entities.

This is an excerpt form my book ***The Colors of Magic***, you might want to check it out if you decide to work with entities.

White Magic is generally done with good intent for the practitioner and the receiver if you are doing it upon request for another. The receiver grants permission.

Grey Magic is generally done with good intent and for help, but the receiver may not be aware the practitioner is doing magic for them. Permission may not necessarily be granted by the receiver.

Black Magic is supposedly done against the receiver and without his knowledge. Generally, it is said that black magic is done to harm and is for selfish purposes. I personally disagree with both those statements.

Permission, understanding, and intent are key words when using magic. Intent is powerful because if your intent is not strong, your magic will not be strong. Your intent must be spot on for magic to work. I believe most people who dabble in magic fully understand the outcomes and consequences. However, with black magic the receiver may not understand what is happening to him. Here again, under certain circumstances I have no problem with this because there is no help for some people and in those cases, you have to do what you have to do. So long as you protect yourself and understand there may be consequences, I don't see a problem. I banish, bind, curse, and hex when I must.

By all means, practice, practice, practice! And, log your journey. When you find your niche, you will know you are home.

Finally, when you become adept at working with the Familiars, Thought Forms & Energy Balls, you may find you have a favorite. Mine is Thought Forms.

Tools of the Trade

Your tools are really the basic tools you use for most of your magic. Candles, pentagram-pentacle, Book of Shadows, wand, representatives of the elements, earth, wind, fire, and water, athame, incense, chalice, and an altar cloth. And, any miscellaneous items depending on the kind of entity you are attempting to create. Or, you may feel tools are unnecessary. The one thing you need though, is your mind and the belief in your creation.

Glossary

I want to familiarize you with some words that may be intimidating for beginners regarding the study and use of Wicca, Paganism, and magic. Some people may disagree with these very basic definitions of words associated with magic, but I keep things simple. Throughout this book, words, and phrases I feel are important are bolded, so pay special attention to those words and phrases. If anything piques your interest, feel free to do a more thorough research. I have learned to take things in stride and use what works for me to keep life less complicated. There are of course many more words and terms associated with the craft. The words in this glossary are for beginners.

Abracadabra: A mystic word used when doing incantations, spells, or even during rituals. Typically, this word is used by magicians when performing magic tricks on stage. Also, it was used in olden times to ward off illness, misfortune, and or harm. *Some may say this has no place when practicing the craft, however it can, especially if it has meaning to you. I use the word with intensity when I point two fingers, my middle and pointer finger at someone or something as I say words like ENOUGH!

Altar: An altar is your sacred space. You decide where your altar is located and what goes on it. Generally, whatever you feel connected to, or whatever tools move you, is what should go on your altar. An altar is very personal.

Alexandrian Witch: An Alexandrian Witch is part of a movement founded in the 1960's called Alexandrian Wicca. This movement is connected to Gardnerian Wicca but uses Qabalah and ceremonial magic as well.

Amulet: An object that is used to attract luck or positive energy. It can be worn or placed on your altar or any location where it may be needed.

Anointing Oil: Oil that has been charged (see charging) and blessed. Anointing oil can be made from a variety of oils depending on the spell work being done. It is considered sacred. Anointing oil is consecrated oil and is used for specific purposes depending on the oil. For example, oil for charging candles for a prosperity spell are cinnamon, myrrh and frankincense.

Augury Witch: A witch who works between cosmic forces and a person on a spiritual quest.
Banish: When you banish something or someone, you send it away.
Banishing: The act of driving away negativity, evil, negative conditions, even negative people. Banishing spells are used to drive away anything you think of as a threat or a nuisance be that a person, obstacle, debt, disease, or even negative habits such as smoking, alcohol or drug use.
Beltane: The Sabbat celebrated on the first day of May.
Besom: The besom is a broom you use to sweep away negative energy. I have two Besoms; one is sprinkled with cinnamon which is a powerful spice used in many potions. By sweeping away negative energy you are in effect blessing and protecting the space you have swept. You should always sweep your circle before you do spell work.
Binding: The act of restricting actions, binding can be positive or negative. You can bind something to you or bind it so that it cannot come near you. Binding can be used with people, objects, places, or even situations. For example, you can bind yourself to your job so that you cannot lose it. Binding is about

restricting, controlling, and stopping certain things from happening.
Black Magic: Black magic is usually considered magic that is used to draw evil spirits to do your bidding.
Black Moon: The black moon is the dark moon.
Blood Moon: October full moon.
Blue Moon: Generally, a blue moon is an extra full moon occurring over the period of a month. It is an extra full moon.
Book of Shadows: A BOS is a book of your own creation. It is used to transcribe your work such as spells, rituals, and what worked as well as what didn't work. It is something you create. It is your Wiccan journal.
Casting a Circle: You cast a circle when doing spell work. The circle is your sacred space. It is swept with your Besom and can be charged with anointing oil. Use whatever oil goes with the spell work you are attempting. The circle is filled with the energy you put into it with your intent. So, give it your all. The more you energize your circle the more powerful your spell work will be.
*I use chalk for drawing my circle. You can purchase a big tub of large sticks of colored chalk and use them for this purpose.

Cauldron: A cauldron can be as simple as a bowl. It does not have to be a huge black pot set up on a tripod and bubbling over a fire. But, if you want to use a black cast-iron pot and place it on a tripod, then by all means do so. If something you already possess moves you to use it as a cauldron, then bless it, charge it, and use it. Find a bowl that feels right to you. I have a copper bowl set aside for that purpose.
Centering: Centering is achieved by meditating before a ritual is performed. It is essential to be centered and focused before beginning any magic work.
Ceremonial Witch: A Ceremonial Witch practices ceremonies and rituals by the book.
Ceremony: A ceremony can be considered a religious, sacred, or a formal event. Rituals and spell work can be ceremonial. By making your spell work ceremonial you are adding more intent.
Chalice: A chalice is one of many tools used during spell work. It can be a talisman, it can be used on your altar, or it can be used as an amulet.
Chant: Chanting can be used to charge your spells. By chanting a spell your mind goes into a meditative state. Your spell become melodious and you tend to concentrate on the spell leaving

the outside world behind. This adds intent to your spell.

Chaos Magic: In my opinion, Chaos Magic and Eclectic Witchery go hand in hand. Using chaos magic, you are merely taking from different types of magic and using the approach that works for you. In Chaos Magic, it is your belief in what you are doing that achieves the results, not the ceremony leading up to it.

Charge: Charge a talisman using the sun, moon, salt, or a ritual as simple as passing the talisman through a candle flame. You may charge an item by chanting, meditating, or dancing. Purified water may also be used to charge your talisman. Remember to create a ritual by saying something like by my power you are charged and empowered to work for me, so it must be. When you charge an item, you are energizing it for a specific purpose.

Charm: A charm is both physical and mental. Physically it is a talisman or amulet and is worn as jewelry or is used to create tools of the trade. Mentally charm is focusing the mind to obtain a desired outcome. Both types of charm can be used in casting spells and doing rituals. Wiccans use charms to attract or repel certain energies to bring about a desired changes and outcomes.

Chaste Moon: March full moon.

Circle: A Circle is a group of people that come together to perform magic. Or, it can be a sacred space you create to do your own magic.
*Again, I create my own circles with colored chalk.
Cleanse: When you cleanse an object, you are preparing it to use in your spell work. Cleansing rids the object of all negativity. Cleansing may also be done to your circle, altar, and sacred space. It goes without saying you want to cleanse yourself as well to send any negative energy on its way before you perform your magic. You may also use a sage cleanse by passing an object through sage smoke, or dancing around your circle or sacred space with the sage.
*Cinnamon is a great spice to use for cleansing.
Cold Moon: December full moon.
Corn Moon: August full moon, also known as the Green Plant full moon.
Coven: A coven is a gathering or community of witches. A high Priest and Priestess usually rule over a coven, and there are usually thirteen members, but there can be more Coven members gather to train, to perform rituals, and celebrate Sabbats. You must be initiated into a coven.
*I am not part of a coven.

Crystal Witch: Crystal Witches work with crystals and stones for healing and balancing. They generally have extensive knowledge about stones, rocks, and crystals.
Curse: A curse is performed for reasons such as retaliation, and is usually negative, or fueled by negative energy. Sometimes a person is cursed by another out of jealousy. If you are considering performing a curse, remember the law of do no harm, harm no one, no harm be done because curses can come back to you.
Cursing: Performing a curse, thought to be manipulative magic.
Dark Moon: The dark moon phase occurs when the moon cannot be seen due to the way it is situated in relation to the Earth.
Dianic Witch: A Dianic Witch practices by calling on the Goddess Diana. They pay homage to all of Diana's aspects, maiden, mother, and crone.
Divination: Divination is the act of foretelling the future, or to gain insight about a situation.
Dowsing: When dowsing, you are doing a type of divination to locate specific objects. Generally, some type of divining rod is used when dowsing.
Draconian Witch: Draconian Witches practice dragon magic.

Draw: When drawing in magic, the witch is attempting to draw a certain kind of energy to the person or situation. A drawing spell is used to bring energy to the practitioner. You may want to draw abundance, love, or health to yourself or someone or something.
Dream Journal: A dream journal is simply a journal you keep near your bed in order to transcribe your dreams upon awakening when they are still fresh on your mind. Dreams can be recurrent. They can give you messages, warnings, or needed information. Some people use dream pillows that contain herbs that enhance dreams. Dream work is important because dreams can provide needed information to your waking life.
*My dreams are vivid, so I keep a journal and pen beside my bed.
Dress: By dressing an object in spell work, you are preparing it for use with your ritual. You may use sage smoke, oils, or trinkets, or all three. With oils, you prepare the oil for the spell, and rub the candle with the oil. When dressing a candle, you are imprinting your intention upon the candle.
Dressing Oil: Dressing oil is a specially prepared oil applied to spell and ritual objects before using them to sanctify, charge and

prepare them for use or after assembling them to charge and activate them. This is called "dressing" or "fixing" the object.
Druid: Druidic Witches focus on Mother Earth in their practice. They do their work in wooded parks and forests. They are nature based. They are in touch with super-natural spirits as part of their craft.
Eclectic Witch: Eclectic witches do not follow any certain religion or practice. Generally, they are intuitive and work from there. They have studied many schools-of-thought and work from all of them.
Effigy: An effigy is an image created or bought that is not drawn. It is an image that is used to resemble a person or an entity. A voodoo doll is an example of an effigy. It is used in spell work and is generally destroyed after it is used.
Elemental Witch: An Elemental Witch is a witch who primarily works with the elements.
Energy Ball: An Energy Ball is a ball of energy formed by you and sent out to the universe to do your bidding.
Energy Work: Energy work is done to change the energy in the energy field. For example, we do energy work to get rid of negativity. When sweeping or circle we are doing energy work.

Chanting and meditating also is a form of energy work.
Equinox: The equinox occurs twice a year. There is an autumnal and vernal equinox. During an equinox daylight and darkness are even.
Esbat: Esbats are times of spiritual gatherings for a coven. Spell work, and or worship take place when the coven gathers together. This usually happens on a full moon.
Essence: The essence of something is the truest nature of that thing, the essence defines the quality of a thing and determines the character of it.
Essential Oil: Essential oils are fragrant oils that come from plants and are used in spell work.
*I keep the main essential oils on hand for charging.
Evil: Evil is a dark concept that is generally thought to be a force of darkness and destruction.
Evil Eye: The evil eye is a look that is given to project a curse, or a feeling of disruption. It is done by staring at a person and sending vibes. You can also create or purchase an evil eye to repel negative energy.

Evocation: Invoking a spirit or a deity. Calling it into spell work, bringing it to the forefront.
Exorcism: An exorcism takes place when an evil entity or negative energy needs to be expelled from a person or a place.
Faerie Witch: Faerie Witches seek information from faery folk and nature spirits as part of their practice.
Familiar: A familiar is a helper, a servant used in spell work or magic. It is generally in the form of an animal. Familiars are bonded to the person they serve, but they tend to have their own personalities. For example, my familiar is my cat named Lola. She came to me through some rather strange circumstances.
*Lola's picture is on my author profile page at the beginning of this book.
Fire Bowl: A fire bowl is used for containing a fire. It is generally propped up on a stand and is used during spell work. Fire bowls can be used indoors (if they are small) or outdoors. Fire bowls are good for burning effigies or lists once a spell is complete.
Full Moon: The moon phase where the entire moon is illuminated and can be seen. This usually occurs once per month.
Forces of nature: Air, earth, water, and fire are the forces of nature invoked in spell work.

Each force is used for a different reason and is associated with a different condition. The forces of nature are also part of the pentagram and or pentacle.

Gaggle of Witches: A gaggle is a group of witches that lacks organization.

Gardnerian Witch: Generally, these witches follow Gerald Gardner's kind of Wicca that emerged in the 1950's. Gerald Gardner is known as the father of Wicca. Gardnerian Witches must be initiated before they can become true Gardnerian Witches.

Gray Witch: Gray witches practice a balanced kind of witchcraft, between white and black magic.

Green Witch: A Green Witch practices by communicating with Mother Earth. She uses tools made from natural materials. She focuses on nature.

Grimoire: You have probably seen and or heard the word Grimoire. In movies, it is a book that appears to be magical and mystical, and even somewhat secretive. A Grimoire is a book akin to a textbook that contains information about magic, spells, potions, rituals, and well you get the idea. The difference between a Grimoire and a Book of Shadows is the Grimoire is the work of one or many persons who authored it, and a Book of Shadows is your own creation. You may certainly use a Grimoire for information, and there are many out there, just as there are many websites where you may find information.

Grounding: Grounding is the process of connecting with and becoming aware of our physical body and how it is connected to the Earth. It allows us to drain negative energy into the Earth as we draw good energy back to us. Grounding helps you to equalize your energy so you can focus while doing your spiritual work. Grounding allows us to eliminate excess energy.

Handfasting: Handfasting is a magic ritual that binds two people together for a specific time frame.

Hare Moon: May moon.

Harvest Moon: The harvest moon is a full moon that occurs at the autumnal equinox.

Hay Moon: July full moon, also known as the Mead moon.

Hearth Witch: Similar to a Kitchen Witch.

Hedge Witch: A Hedge Witch travels between worlds. She communicates with the spiritual realm delivering messages between worlds.

Herbs: Herbs are woody plants that flower and are used in spell work.

Hereditary Witch: A Hereditary Witch is born into the practice. Her family members have passed down their craft from generation to generation.
Hex: A hex is a curse that is put on a person or a place. It is spell work that can be negative.
Hexing: Performing a hex.
Imbolc: The Sabbat celebrated around the second day of February.
Incantation: A group of words created to cast a spell. Though not connected to any specific religion, incantations are used in many religions. Incantations are often thought of as being enchanting because they are used to create a desired effect. They can be spoken or sung. They can be intoxicating and put the person reciting the incantation in a spell-like state.
Incense: Incense is a fragrant material that produces smoke and is used in spell work. It can be used by itself or with herbs and oils.
Initiation: Initiation is the ceremony when a person is admitted to a coven. It is not necessary to join a coven. But if you choose to do so you will go through an initiation ceremony.
Intent: Intent is the basis of magical spell work. Intent is resolve and determination. The stronger the intent, the better your chance for

success when doing spell work. Intent is serious eager attention you put into your spell work.
Invoke: Invoking is to summon, bring forth, or draw a spirit or deity you can communicate with.
Karma: The belief that what you do, your thoughts, your actions come back to you. Karma can be good or bad. It is part of your spiritual path.
Kitchen Witch: A Kitchen Witch uses practicality in her craft. She works with recipes and potions. Her home is her sacred place.
Lammas: The harvest Sabbat celebrated in August.
Litha: The Sabbat celebrated as the summer solstice around June twenty-first.
Lunar Day: Lunar day begins when the moon rises and ends when the moon sets. Knowing when this occurs can benefit spell work.
Lunar Eclipse: A lunar eclipse occurs during a full moon. The sun, earth, and moon are in alignment. occurs when the Sun, Earth and Moon are in syzygy or perfect (or near perfect) alignment. Lunar eclipse spell work is powerful.
Lunar Witch: A lunar Witch follows lunar cycles as she practices her rituals.
Mabon: The Sabbat celebrated as the Autumn Equinox around September twenty-first.

Magic: Magic is neither religious nor scientific. Throughout history magic has conjured up negative and positive connotations, depending on the century, and the ideology of the faction in charge. Magic is the use of personal power to bring about change, to the physical world. Magic is brought forth by a person's will, his belief in his power. Wicca and magic go hand in hand. Wiccans use magic. While some believe magic is evil, paranormal, or super-natural, people who use magic believe it is available to anyone who believes in the power of his own mind. There is nothing abnormal about it, it is merely using and channeling personal power with or without the use of aids or tools. It is a natural force. You can't see it, you can't touch it, but once you get good at it, you can feel it when it's working! Believe in magic, or don't believe in it, either way for you personally you're right.

Magical Petitions: Magical petitions are simply written spell work. Generally, the desire is written on some type of paper, sealed, and after the spell is activated, it is released by fire in a burning bowl, or buried. It can also be saved in your BOS (Book of Shadows). It can be a single spell or part of a bigger spell that has many parts. I generally write my desires, meditate over them, then burn them and release the ashes outdoors to the U. I find that writing my desires makes me concentrate more deeply and my intent becomes stronger.

Magick: The same as magic defined below. However, the spelling was changed so people wouldn't confuse stage magic by magicians with practitioners of paranormal magic associated with Pagan type religions.

Manipulative magic: Magic that is done against a person without their permission, because it may impact their free will.

Meditation: A process of turning inward, quieting the mind, and reflecting. Meditation is a time you set aside to gather yourself, to renew and recharge yourself.

Mojo Bag: A mojo bag is a small bag containing magical items that are charged and used during spell work. The bag contains specific items depending on the spells. A witch can have more than one mojo bag.

Necromancy: Necromancy is used in spell work to contact and communicate with the dead. It is believed the dead can provide insights into situations that the living cannot see, such as foretelling future events.

New Moon: The new moon is the moon phase that usually cannot be seen from Earth or appears as a slight slender crescent. See dark moon.

Nocturnal Witch: A Nocturnal Witch works at night and draws her powers from the darkness.

Occult: Simply put, the occult is the study of paranormal, metaphysical, mystical, magical, and or super-natural events. The very word occult tends to take on an evil or negative feeling. There is nothing evil about study the occult.

Omen: An omen is a sign of something to come, an event that may be positive or negative. In your study of Wicca, you may get 'feelings' of something that is about to happen. Or, you may have dreams about something that is about to happen. Your omens are your omens. Omens have different meanings for different people. If an event occurs every time you see or find something—that may be an omen. It could be something as simple as finding a feather.

Ostara: The Sabbat celebrated as the Spring Equinox on March twenty-first.

Out of Body Experience: An OBE is an out-of-body experience. It simply means your soul travels outside your body. This frequently happens when a person is sleeping, or in a dream state. People have reported out-of-body experiences when in an accident, undergoing surgery, or in a dangerous situation. An out-of-body experience can be intentional (through meditation) or accidental (such as leaving the body during a traumatic experience).

Pagan: Pagan covers a lot of different faiths, usually earth based. Pagans follow a spiritual path centered in nature. Most Pagans are polytheistic. That is, they believe in many deities.

Pair Moon: June full moon.

Pendulum: A pendulum is an object attached to yarn, string, chain, or even wire. It can be any type of object, but should be something that you relate to, something that you connect with on a deeper level. It is used for both dowsing and divining. To use the pendulum, you hold it over something and concentrate. The pendulum swings in a certain direction which will then give you the answer to your question. For example, a pendulum held over a pregnant woman's body that swings a certain way can predict the sex of the baby. But the pendulum has no power of its own, the answer is coming from the subconscious of the person holding the pendulum. You have the power, and the answer is coming through you.

Pentacle: A pentacle is a five-pointed star, the points represent spirit, earth, air, water, and fire. It is encased in a circle. The pentacle is used in magic for spell-work. It can also be made into jewelry and worn.
Pentagram: The pentagram is also called a pentacle, and like the pentacle is a religious symbol for Pagans. The star has five points, the top point of the pentagram represents Spirit, this is where all the elements come together. The upper right is water, the upper left is air, the lower right is fire, and the lower left is earth. The pentagram like the pentacle is used for spell-work. It can be placed on your altar, or it can be your altar if you do not have a dedicated altar. You of course have to charge your pentagram with your energy when doing spell work. You can also buy jewelry in the shape of a pentagram and wear it for whatever purpose you decide.
Personal Power: Personal power is the power that emanates through you to perform your magic.
Poppet: Poppets and voodoo dolls are used interchangeably. The dolls are made in the image of the individual of the spell you are creating. If you make your own poppet, you can use it for love, prosperity, to overcome illness,

protection, banishing, or binding. Once the poppet has been used, and the spell has been accomplished, the doll should be disposed of properly. A poppet can be an amulet, or a talisman. The dolls can be made from several different materials. I use sticks, moss, and material to create my dolls. I use a variety of trinkets to make my dolls specific for the purpose it represents.

Pow-Wow Witch: Pow-Wow witches are rooted in Pennsylvania and practice a type of Germanic witchcraft that is over 400 years old. They focus on healing rituals and spells.

Purification: Purification ceremonies are performed to clear away negativity, undesired influences, bad energy, or anything that invades you or your space. People who practice the craft use purification ceremonies to clear the way for their ceremonies or rituals. They not only clean their workspace, they also purify themselves, and their tools, such as wands, pendulums, candles, bowls, and anything used during their spells, rituals, and ceremonies.

*If you use water for purification you can use water you have left out in a container during a full moon, so it becomes charged with the moon's energy.

Religion: A set of beliefs that usually honors a higher power.
Religious Witch: A Religious Witch may follow a religion in accordance with her witchcraft practices.
Ritual: A ritual is a ceremony that is generally done the same way all the time. Rituals are done during particular events such as Sabbats, or even moon phases. Rituals Are beneficial because they help you in being consistent in the craft.
Ritual Ceremony: A ceremony performed to achieve desired effects, where your spell work is practiced.
Ritual Tools: The tools used to accomplish your desired effects from the ritual or spell you are accomplishing.
Rod: A rod is a wand, stick, staff, or even metal that is straight and is used in spell work. Rods are also used in divining.
*I use a carved walking stick that belonged to my father when I need a rod.
Sabbat: The Sabbats are special holidays. Generally, there are four or eight Sabbats that are celebrated throughout the year. The four main Sabbats are Samhain, Yule (the winter solstice), Imbolc, Ostara, Beltane, Litha (the summer solstice), Lammas, and Mabon (the

autumnal equinox). Each Sabbat is a holiday, a feast day and a celebration day.

Sachet: Sachets are small cloth bags that contain herbs, spices, talismans, and or amulets that are made and used for spell work. They can be used for protection, attraction, or banishing. Sachet bags can be made out of many materials and colors. They can be solid or made from netting. The materials you use to fill the sachet bags should be in accordance with your spells. For example, if you are carrying a sachet bag to attract money, it should be gold or green, and you may want to put coins in it.

Sacred Space: Your sacred space is the space you have set aside for your craft. It can be indoors or outdoors. It doesn't have to be an entire room; it may be a corner where you place your altar. If you choose not to have a sacred space, that's alright as well. I have an area in my home-office where I keep my tools. But I do the majority of my rituals and spells outdoors on my patio in my backyard. The important thing to remember is that whenever you do rituals or spell work, you will need to purify and charge your space.

Samhain: The Sabbat celebrated around November first and considered the first day of Winter.

Scrying: Scrying is accomplished by using tools such as crystal balls. You meditate, then gaze into the crystal ball to see visions of past or future events. Some people use water and glass as well as crystal. It is a form of divining.
Scrying Mirror: A mirror may be used for scrying. It can be a reflective mirror or a black mirror. You use a scrying mirror the same way you use a crystal ball. You may see images in the mirror from the past or future. It is a form of divining.
*I have a tortoise shell mirror that belonged to my mother that I use for scrying.
Sea Witch: Sea Witches are drawn to Water. Sea Witches focus on moon lore and the ebb and flow of the tide. They are attuned to the weather in their practice.
Seed Moon: April full moon.
Shaman: Shamans are able to alter their state-of-mind and work from that altered state. They are able to communicate on the spiritual realm when in trance. They work with divination and healing and can channel messages.
Shielding: Shielding techniques are used to protect yourself or others from negative energy by creating a barrier to block the negativity.
Sigil: A sigil is a drawn symbol used in spell work. Sigils represent prosperity, money, love,

protection, and a host of other conditions. You may carry a sigil with you the same way you would an amulet or a talisman. You can find sigils online, but here again I believe the ones you create yourself are more effective because of the energy you are putting into the creation as you work. Sigils may be used as your signature on letters, emails, and cards. You can also create a special sigil for your altar.

Smoke cleansing: Smoke cleansing is accomplished by using incense, or herbs. It is a purification process.

Smudge: Smudging is another purification process. You use a smudge stick to cleanse your home or even your body of negative or unwanted energy. I smudge with sage monthly, or when I feel negative energy in my home.

Snow Moon: November full moon.

Solar Eclipse: A solar eclipse occurs at the time of the new moon. The moon passes between the earth and the sun blocking the sun. There are total and partial eclipses.

Solitary Witch: A solitary is a witch who works alone. She does not belong to any group.

Solstice: A solstice occurs twice a year. There is a summer and a winter solstice. The summer solstice is the longest day of the year with sunlight. The winter solstice is the shortest day of the year to receive sunlight. At the time of the summer solstice the sun has moved to its highest point in the sky just as in the winter it is the lowest point in the sky (from the horizon).

Spell: A spell is something that is cast to bring about something desired, material, spiritual, or a condition. Spells are focused energy. Spells are written and or spoken words. Speaking your spell aloud is important especially when it is repeated in a meditative state. You can chant your spell as many times as you feel necessary, you will know when you are finished. I write my own spells in four-line rhymes because this is what works for me. Four-line rhymes are easy to remember and chant. They also tend to become like a song when I am chanting them, and I believe that adds more energy to what I am attempting to achieve. It is important to remember to do your spells with focused intent. Your intent is what drives your spell.

Spell Craft: Spell craft is the craft of writing, and casting spells. Again, you may create your own spells, or use spells you've read in books or online. I believe that crafting my own spells and crafting my own materials I use in my magic work gives my work more power.

Spirit: Spirit is non-physical. It is of higher consciousness. It is the top point of the pentagram where all the forces come together. In religion spirit is all there is. In a human spirit is the essence, the energy, we are spirit in a physical human body. The body ceases to exist but spirit lives on.

Spirit Animal: A spirit animal is an animal claimed by a human to be their guide. It is the essence of the animal. For example, a tiger may be your spirit animal. If so, you as the human exude the essence of a tiger.

Spirit world: Wiccans, witches, practitioners of magic generally accept the spirit world as real. They usually accept an afterlife and have no problem contacting the spirit world.

Stang: A tree or a forked branch used during rituals or on an altar.

Statement of Intent: A statement of intent is the spoken purpose of a spell. A spell begins with a statement of intent. The intent is the power behind the spell. The stronger the intent, the stronger the spell will be. A statement of intent is generally a positive statement. The very foundation of spell work begins with a statement of intent by the person performing the spell.

Storm Moon: February full moon.

Subconscious Mind: The subconscious mind is the part of the mind that functions below the conscious mind.
Summerland: Where the body goes to rest in Paganism. Also known as the land of the dead.
Supermoon: A supermoon is used to describe a full or new moon that occurs when the moon is in the closest position to the Earth. A supermoon happens from three to five times a year.
Sword: A sword is a tool used to direct energy. It is similar to using a wand, or a staff. Again, the energy it wields is the energy you, the practitioner put into it, you must charge the sword the same way you would charge any tool you use in your craft.
Sympathetic Magic: Like attracts like, used in spell work to accomplish your intent.
Taglock: An item used in spell. Something that links to the spell. In a banishing spell you may use something that belongs to the person you are banishing as part of the spell. If you were to write the person's name on paper, you might fold something into the paper and then burn it as you say your incantation that banishes the person from your life. *See banishing.
Talisman: A talisman is an object that the user believes holds magical properties that bring

good luck to the possessor or protect the possessor from evil or harm. A talisman usually has to be charged to hold magical powers. A talisman may be worn, carried in a mojo bag, placed on an altar, or brought out during spell work.

Thoughtform: Thoughtforms are bundles of psychic energy created by a magic practitioner to work for them.

Threefold Law: The rule of three basically states that whatever energy a person puts forth whether negative or positive will come back to that person in threes. Think of it as karma three times.

Tincture: A tincture is made using some type of alcohol and herbs. You can make your own tinctures using herbs and any type of alcohol preferably 100 proof such as Everclear or vodka. I use Everclear for my tinctures. Place your herb (your choice) in a mason jar, then pour the Everclear (or alcohol of choice) in the jar, and seal it. I let my tinctures sit for a year before opening the jar. When you do open the jar, strain the mixture into a clean jar, and seal again. Tinctures can be taken under the tongue (internally). General a few drops are all that is necessary. If you are going to make and use tinctures, be sure to get more information on what herbs are used for what specific purposes.

Traditional Witch: A Traditional Witch who is Wiccan focuses her practice on her religion.

Uncrossing: Uncrossing is simply removing a curse that has been thrust upon you. You can also use binding and banishing to remove curses.

U: Universe

Vernal Equinox: The vernal equinox is the Spring equinox. It occurs around the twenty first of March.

Visualization: Visualization is the process of forming mental images in your mind. You can also make visualization boards of what you want by cutting pictures and sayings from magazines and pasting them on a board, or cardboard, and meditating on the board for a period of time. People use visualization for creating their world the way they would like it to be. You can use visualization during your spell work instead of chanting.

Voodoo doll: A Voodoo doll is a poppet or effigy used in magic. To some this type of magic is negative. I create and use my own dolls for specific purposes. Voodoo dolls can be a tool for focus when using them in spell work. They can represent people, situations, or desires. I find by using a voodoo doll my intent and focus are sharp.

Wand: A wand is a rod, or a stick, that is used as a tool in your magic. I created my own wand using a cinnamon stick, feathers, yarn, and trinkets that were personal to me. You can create different wands that are used for a variety of reasons. My wand is used for prosperity spells.

Waning Moon: The waning moon is the time when the moon appears to become smaller. The waning moon is a time for decrease and elimination. This is a time to do spell work when you want to eliminate something or someone from your life.

Waxing Moon: The waxing moon is the time when the moon appears to grow in the sky, when it is most visible. The waxing moon is a time for increase and gain. refers to the application of wax on something. Your spell work during the waxing moon would be for situations of gain and increase.

Wheel of the Year: The wheel of the year in Wicca, is a full cycle of each of the four seasons that make up a year.

White Witch: White witches practice goodness and benevolence in all they do. They do not cast spells that cause harm. They do not

practice any type of selfish magic. White Witches live their life by the Wiccan Rede.
Wicca: Wicca is a religious practice where magic and spell-work are used, but it is not all about magic and spell-work. Wicca has been around throughout recorded history but wasn't always called Wicca. Wicca is nature oriented and considered a religion. Witchcraft and witches are usually associated with Wicca, but not all Wiccans practice witchcraft and not all witches are Wiccan. Wicca has a set of beliefs, and certain holidays it celebrates.
Wiccan: Wiccan is an individual that belongs to the religion called Wicca. Or, it can be used to describe anything related to Wicca, spells, spell work, talismans, objects, rituals, etc.
Wiccan Rede: "And harm ye none, do what ye will."
Widdershins: Moving counterclockwise when performing rituals.
Witch: Generally, a witch is female. A witch is usually associated with the practice of witchcraft. Witches are not necessarily Pagan, or Wiccan, but they certainly can practice both. They can also be Christian or associated with any religious belief. A group of witches who practice together are generally members of a coven. A solitary witch practices alone, and is

not usually a member of a group, or coven. Their practice is usually done in and around their home. An eclectic witch does not follow a specific tradition and is not initiated into a coven. It is a more modern way to practice. Eclectic witches are not near as formal as witches in a coven. Eclectic witches create their own methods, spells, chants, affirmations, incantations, and rituals. But they don't necessarily turn away from traditional tried-and-true methods either. Eclectic witches follow their own path; they create their own magic. They may follow a tradition but aren't bothered if they don't. Most witches follow and use the basics of witchcraft, such as moon charts for spells, candles, herbs, spices, oils, and trinkets.

Witch Doctor: A witch doctor creates his own natural medicines for healing. Witch doctors are deeply spiritual and have a serious respect for nature.

Witchcraft: Witchcraft is a practice, that has a formal set of beliefs. Some people disagree with witchcraft as a religion and call it a set of skills used to practice magic.

Wolf Moon: January full moon.

Yule: The Sabbat celebrated as the Winter solstice around December twenty-first.

Yule Log: The log (legend says use oak) that is burned on Yule.

As you become familiar with this glossary of Wiccan terms, you might check some online sources for more in-depth terms to build your knowledge. The more you learn, the more powerful your magic will become. And by studying and broadening your horizons, you are in effect practicing the craft. You might set your sights on learning something new every day. The more you know, the more you know!

Incantation Glossary

From my first book of this 'beginner' series I have repeatedly told you rhyming ditties work best for me. They are sort of like repeating the invocations used with Rosaries and Mala beads. I in fact use both because I am a hands-on person. Visualization is not my forte! I don't use my Rosary or Mala beads when practicing the craft, but I do use them as a sort of talisman when I am trying to center myself and nothing else is working.

Anyway, all of that aside, I am including a chapter with my rhyming ditties in the beginner books. As you read through these invocations you can see that they may be inter-changeable.

As I go forward with these books, I will add to this chapter much the same as I add to the glossary.

Please, if any of my invocations work for you, feel free to incorporate them in your work. Or, try writing your own. You'd be surprised what you can come up with, and there is something about accomplishment that makes life just a little bit sweeter!

From Book of Shadows

Talisman charge and blessing (Whatever I am blessing goes in the blank, it could be a crystal, a wand, a rock, oil, or whatever I have created)

I bless this ______________________ to the powers that be
all good things now work through me.
Blessed be.

Release someone, a condition, or a situation.

I release _____________________to their—its highest good,
they—it goes their way, and I go my way,
and we are free of each other, and karmic debt.
Blessed be.

House Mortgage

To pay in full
By my magic
I bless this home and everything it holds
Bring me the money, the finance, the means
To own my home on my own.
Blessed be

Immediate need (I use this frequently throughout the day as it pops into my mind.)

Money, money comes to me
It is my will, so it must be.
Blessed be.

Lottery (I play the lottery. I say this when I purchase my ticket. Don't forget to bless your tickets to the power of luck and chance!)

Money, money comes to me
I have won the lottery
Blessed be

Money (For whatever purpose you have in mind)

Money, money blessed be
Bring wealth and riches straight to me
Blessed be

Prosperity (Prosperity is not just money, people prosper in a lot of diverse ways)

Prosperity, prosperity
Find your way to me
Prosperity, prosperity
Bring all that I can see
Blessed be

Extra money for your personal use

A dollar here, a dollar there,

I see dollars everywhere
Make your way into my home
Stay awhile, do not roam
Blessed be

A specific amount you need (a hundred, a thousand, you fill in the amount)

A hundred here, a hundred there
I see money everywhere
Bring my hundreds straight to me
As I need, so it must be
Blessed be

Soul mate (Her can be substituted for him)

Lovely lady of the moon
Bring my soul mate
And bring him soon.
Blessed be.

Family love

The candle burns and lights the way
For family coming home to stay
Blessed be

Friends

Fill my life with friends untold
All that I desire

My world can hold
Blessed be

World (he and brother are not gender specific)

May the world be enfolded in love
From earth below to the heavens above
May all mankind accept one another
Treat everyone like he is your brother
Blessed be

Specific condition (You can put any condition where I put cancer, since I am a cancer survivor, I used cancer)

Hear my plea to the powers that be
Keep my body cancer free
Blessed be.

General

Keep my body healthy and strong
Keep my lifeline forever long
Keep me free from harm and fear
Keep peace and love abiding here
Blessed be.

Success
Success in all I want and need
Comes through my door today

Success in what I want to be
Shines through in all I say.
Blessed be

Happiness

Happiness comes to my life
Be gone anger, stress and fear
I am happy, and free from strife
Negativity can't come near
Blessed be

Rejuvenating happiness

Lovely lady of the moon
Take away my pain
Lovely lady of the moon
Make me happy once again
Blessed be

Everything spell (I desire)

Success beyond my wildest dreams
Wealth beyond my wildest schemes
Love and health fulfilled desires
My life becomes all I aspire
Blessed be

From Moon Phase Rituals Made Easy

Luna Luna work with me
Show me what I need to see
Bring to light what I might do
So, I may be blessed like you.
Blessed be

Moon of darkness
Moon of light
Help me find
My way tonight
Blessed be

Mother moon shining bright
Help me see my way tonight
Share your power, strength, and light
Make it happen, make it right
Blessed be

Lovely Luna rising high
Lighting up the nighttime sky
Remove my barriers, darkness, and pain
Make my life grow light again
Blessed be

Oh, bright and silvery moon on high
Lighting up the nighttime sky
Fill my life with riches untold

All you deliver I can hold
Blessed be

From Sabats and Esbats Made Easy

Spells of **Imbolc** can focus on cleansing the home, spirit, and body, include love in these spells.

May the powers that be bless this home
Making it sacred, pure and clean
Let nothing but love, joy and happiness
Enter by sights and forces unseen
Blessed be

Spells of **Ostara** can focus on the arrival of Spring, rebirth, new beginnings, and fertility.

Blessings of newness and fertility abound
Making the environment lush
Let nothing but balance, hope, and renewal
Light up the days and the nights.
Blessed be

Spells of **Beltane** can focus on the beginning of the planting season.

Bless this ground by the Powers that be
So the seeds of my spirit can grow
Let nothing negative block my way
So my words of power don't sway.
Blessed be

Spells of **Litha** revolve around the Summer Solstice and the longest day and shortest night of the year.

Bless this day the Powers that be
Let our time be joyous and filled with play
Set our spirits free to fly high and wide
As we thank you for blessings, we abide
Blessed be

Spells of **Lammas** revolve around the first harvest of the Summer.

Bless this day the Powers that be
Let our time be joyous and filled with play
Set our spirits free to fly high and wide
As we thank you for blessings, we abide
Blessed be

Spells of **Mabon**, Autumn has arrived. Daylight is waning, and it's getting darker earlier.

Bless this time as the colors change
The season is rich, in bounty and beauty
Lay all negativity aside
By the power of three abide.
Blessed be

Spells for **Samhain** can revolve around your connection to people and the environment.

Spirits protect me and those I love
Both here and now and in between
Keep my spirit alive and well
And bless the house in which I dwell.
Blessed be

Spells of **Yule**. Center your spells and incantations around home and hearth. Family and friends are important now.

Lords and ladies and powers that be
Bless my home, my friends and family.
The season is joyous, and I am well
By the power of three in my heart please dwell.
Blessed be

From Banishing, Binding, Cursing, and Hexing

I ***banish*** ______________ *(name of person)*
You brought discord into my life
And caused me turmoil and pain
My life holds no place for you
You will never affect me again.
Blessed be

I ***banish*** _______________ *(a condition or situation)*
My life has no room for you
Release your hold on me
Move on, be gone, withdraw, depart
As I begin anew and restart.
Blessed be

I ***bind*** ______________ *(insert name)*
You will never cross my path again
Or cause me hurt and pain
I bind you left, I bind you right,
You're gone forever more.
Blessed be

I ***bind*** ______________ *(a condition or situation)*
I bind you today, I bind you tonight
I bind you left, I bind you right.
I bind you tight, no more to be,
I bind you gone away from me.

Blessed be.

I ***bind*** __________________ *(behavior)*
I bind your conduct,
It stops today
Hear me, don't test me
Or I'll send you away.
Blessed be.

I ***curse*** *you* ____________________ *(name or condition)*
I curse you here, I curse you now
I curse you forever more
Stay away from me and mine
For I now close that door.
Blessed be

I **hex** ______________________ (fill in the person or condition)
I cast this hex upon you
You shall endure all that you have placed on me
I cast this hex upon you
You shall never more be free.
Blessed be

I ***hex*** *you* _____________________ *(name or condition)*
May you forever suffer what you brought upon me
May you never know how my pain felt

May all your days be burdened
With what you have dealt.
Blessed be.

From What kind of Witch are you¿

My light is shining deep inside
Using healthy ways, I do abide
The flame that burns within my soul
Heals me now and makes me whole.
Blessed be

Joy and happiness come into my life
Be gone anger, be gone strife
I am healthy, happy, and free
My life holds no anxiety.
Blessed be

My garden grows so healthily
Providing healing herbs for me
My food is pure and chemical free
I gladly share my endless bounty.
Blessed be

My besom works its charm for me
I'm sweeping away negativity.
Blessed be

Fill my life with prosperity untold
All I desire
My life can hold.
Blessed be

Fire burning hot and red
Comes through for me today.
Burn away the things I ask
Take my troubles away.
Blessed be

Negative energy go away
This fire burns so you won't stay
My family and home is happy and strong
Be gone now, you do not belong.
Blessed be

Bless my home
Oh lord I pray
Keep it safe by night and day.
Keep us happy, healthy and free
I ask of you three by three.
Blessed be

Earth and air,
Wind and fire,
Drive away all harm and fear
So only love may abide in here.
Blessed be

You borrowed money you agreed to repay
You owe and you know there' nothing left to say.
You've had plenty of time to make things right
May you suffer financially til you see the light.

So mote it be

Lovely lady of the sea
Bring forth your watery mystery.
Help me see the way to go
I bow to your power'
Make it so.
Blessed be

From earth to my kitchen
I grind you fine
With love and care
I'm happy to share.
May my herbs bring all you need
To heal your soul in thought and deed.
Blessed be

What I lost
Help me find
Between the realms
Of thought and mind.
Blessed be

From Centering, Grounding, and Shielding

Centering Invocation

I come together here and now
Body, mind, and soul unite
With intent my forces blend
Working together to the end.
Harming none and blessing all,
Hear me now, heed my call.
Blessed be

Grounding Invocation

Mother Earth, nature, nurture
Let your energy fill my soul.
Ground me now and ground me well
Keep me stable, shored and quell.
Harming none and blessing all,
Hear me now, heed my call.
Blessed be

Shielding Invocation

Crystals, mirrors, gestures, words
Protect me from unwelcome forces.
Shields up with intent I'm charmed

I am blessed and can't be harmed.
Harming none and blessing all,
Hear me now, heed my call.
Blessed be

From The Elements

Spells or incantations for Spirit

All that is holy, heavenly and sublime
Protect my circle against forces unwelcome.
Spirit divine charm and bless me
And keep me free from harm as I
Harm none and bless all.

Spells or incantations for Water

Rivers, oceans, streams and lakes,
Flood my circle with welcome forces.
Surge me with intent, bewitch me
As I carry on my desire
I am blessed and can't be harmed.
Hear me now, heed my call.
Blessed be

Spells or incantations for Fire

Mother Earth, nature, nurture
Let your fire fill my soul.
Fuel me full and well and now
Inflame my desire, inflame it well
Harming none and blessing all,
Hear me now, heed my call.
Blessed be

Spells or incantations for Earth

Mother Earth I beseech you
Come into my circle and
Protect me from uninvited forces.
Help keep my intentions pure,
Shore up my resolve,
I'm blessed and can't be damaged.
Nor will I damage none
Hear me now, hear my call.
Blessed be

Spells or incantations for Air

I call to you here and now
Oh great element of air.
With intent my forces blend
With your swirling forces
Working together to the end.
Harming none and blessing all,
Hear me now, heed my call.
Blessed be

From The Colors of Magic

Spells or incantations for Gray Magic

On this paper, in the center I state my fear
I now send if far away from me and here
I will not veer from my quest nor fate
I now banish forever that which holds me back
I rebuke the fear and take my life back.

Spells or incantations for Black Magic

You messed with me, now I'll mess with you
This is what this witch must do.
You'll feel it all to soon.
You'll stay clear of me, I've seen to that,
You're finished, be gone, get away from me, scat.

Spells or incantations for White Magic

All powers that come from the East
Assist me now as I claim what's mine.
Grant me resplendent health,
Let My life force shine through
So that I may have unending wellbeing.

From Sigils and Chaos Magic

All powers from the universe
Assist me now as I claim what's mine.
I welcome the energies air, earth, wind, fire, and spirit
To infuse their vitality into my desire.
So mote it be

On this paper I state my desire.
My words drawn out set my soul afire.
Blessed be

From Goddess Magic & Energy

Hail Diana

Goddess of the forests and moon
I devote myself to your feminine wisdom
I honor you and celebrate your spirit.
May my spirit emulate yours
And may my life mimic thee.
I pray these wishes be fulfilled
Goddess, maiden, mother, crone
Diana, enlighten me today, tonight
And every day and night
To know what is right.
Blessed be.

Hail Luna

Lovely Goddess of the moon
Shine your light upon me
Bring me the power to see
To know
To understand
Lady of the moon guide me that I may know
With certainty
Make my wish come true tonight
Bring me my heart's desire
Ever grateful I shall be
Blessed be

Hail Hecate

Hear me Hecate
Goddess of the underworld and crossroads
I devote myself to your feminine wisdom
I honor you and celebrate your spirit.
May my spirit emulate yours
May I learn to embrace and accept change
And the cycles of life.
Light my way with your torches
That I may see the way clearly
I pray these wishes be fulfilled
Goddess, maiden, mother, crone
Hecate, enlighten me at this crossroads
At which I find myself.
And every day and night
To know what is right.
Blessed be

Hail Brighid

Goddess of fire, light, and the stirrings of Spring.
I devote myself to your feminine wisdom
I honor you and celebrate your spirit.
May my spirit emulate yours
May I learn to embrace and accept change
Show me the way to light the flame
Of my creativity.
That I may see the way clearly

I pray these wishes be fulfilled
Goddess Brighid, heal me and enlighten me
With your radiance and higher intellect
That I may emulate your ways.
Hear me Brighid Goddess of the hearth
That my home, my soul, may burst with your
Enlightenment and healing ways.
Blessed be.

Hail Demeter

Goddess of the bountiful harvest
I beg of you to hear me as I ask you
To bestow your blessings here and now
Help me plane new seeds
Help me grow with your wisdom
Help me harvest new ideas
And preserve them evermore.
Demeter, I beg of you to help me understand
The cycles of life and how they unfold.
Help me Demeter as I go through this life
To do no harm, and to learn patience, understanding
And unconditional love.
Blessed be

Hail Isis

Goddess of Earth, water, and sky
I revel in your magic and glories.
Your strength of character

Is my desire.
Beautiful Goddess Isis help me experience
The mysteries of your intuition and knowing.
I honor your abilities
That I may emulate them divine Goddess.
I open myself to rebirth that I may
Be like you oh great Goddess Isis.
Blessed be.

From Energize your Magic with Candles, Herbs, Oils & Stones

*In these incantations I use the name of a candle, herb, oil, or stone. You do not have to do that. It is something that works for me!

Money

This candle burns
Throughout the day
To bring money
To me today
I could use some extra cash
To pay my bills
And restock my stash.
As I will, so it shall be.

Protection

Protect my home and person today
All bad energy be on your way.
Cinnamon, cinnamon do your trick
Take it all away and do it quick.
So mote it be

Health

Powers that be take my illness away

I do not want it here to stay.
I bid it leave my body well
I use this Goldenseal to
Charge my spell
Be gone, so mote it be.

Banish

Stinging Nettle do your trick
Take this negativity away.
Be gone, leave, it cannot stay
As I go about my merry way.
So mote it be

Banishing

You messed with me, now I'll mess with you
This is what this witch must do.
Black Onyx charge and heed what I say
Get rid of all who's in my way.
You'll stay clear of me, now go
It's over, be gone, get away from me stat
So mote it be

*The fourth line you may replace who's with a person or condition.

From Altars, Circles and Sacred Spaces

Dedicated altar blessing

Hail Hecate

Hear me Hecate
Goddess of the underworld and crossroads
I devote myself to your feminine wisdom
I honor you and celebrate your spirit.
May my spirit emulate yours
May I learn to embrace and accept change
And the cycles of life.
Light my way with your torches
That I may see the way clearly
Bless my altar with your wisdom
That it serves me well
In all endeavors.
I pray these wishes be fulfilled
Goddess, maiden, mother, crone
Hecate, enlighten me at this altar
At which I find myself.
And every day and night
To know what is right.
Blessed be

Elemental altar blessings

All that is holy, heavenly and sublime

Protect my circle against forces unwelcome.
Spirit *divine charm and bless me*
And keep me free from harm as I
Harm none and bless all.
Hear me now, heed my call spirit divine
Blessed be

Waters *of the universe,*
Flood my circle with welcome forces.
Surge me with intent, bewitch me
As I carry on my desire
I am blessed and can't be harmed.
Hear me now, heed my call.
Blessed be

Mother Earth, nature, nurture
Let your ***fire*** *fill my soul.*
Fuel me full and well and now
Inflame my desire, inflame it well
Harming none and blessing all,
Hear me now, heed my call.
Blessed be

Mother ***Earth*** *I beseech you*
Come into my circle and
Protect me from uninvited forces.
Help keep my intentions pure,
Shore up my resolve,
I'm blessed and can't be damaged.

Nor will I damage none
Hear me now, hear my call.
Blessed be

I call to you here and now
Oh great element of ***air****.*
With intent my forces blend
With your swirling forces
Working together to the end.
Harming none and blessing all,
Hear me now, heed my call.
Blessed be

Closing circle blessings

I've called upon you ________________ by my will
Earth, air, wind, fire, and spirit
For all your powers that lead my way
I thank you and leave you for now.
*In the blank space if you use the elements, say elements. If you use a Goddess, say her name.

Opening a circle incantation

As I will, my circle is cast
My forces joined with all I invite
My intention is clear
My will is divine
My circle is pure

*You may put in a specific force or forces in the second line and call them aloud.

Closing a circle incantation

As I will my circle has served
My forces recede
My intention is satisfied
My will has been met
Thank you to all who have joined me
Blessed be, my circle is closed.

Sacred space blessing

I call on the forces of Earth, wind, fire and water to bless this space
Keep me safe in my sacred space
Let no harm or negativity enter
I consecrate this space here and now
As mine and the forces I call upon to enter
Blessed be

From Spells, Incantations, Invocations, Evocations & Rituals

Tool cleaning cleanse

I cleanse and consecrate ______________
May your energy bless and bring
Success to my ritual.
So mote it be.

Money incantation

The candles burn
The tools turn
Success now favors me.
I attract the cash I desire
To pay my bills
And restock my stash.
As I will, so it shall be.

Simple Invocation to start all your rituals—

My circle opens
Guide me as I do my work
Guard me at the door
Stay awhile and see me through
Forever I am grateful

Evocation calling on a higher power

Hail Luna
Lovely Goddess of the moon
I call on you to assist me,
Shine your light upon me
Bring me the power to see
To know
To understand
Lady of the moon guide me that I may know
With certainty
Make my wish come true tonight
Bring me my heart's desire
Ever grateful I shall be
Blessed be

From Calling the Quarters

Spells or incantations for Earth-the North Quarter—

Mother Earth I call on you
Come into my circle and
Protect me.
Help keep my intentions pure,
Keep me in your protective hold,
Assist me with your energy
I'm blessed and can't be damaged.
Nor will I damage.
Hear me now, hear my call.
Blessed be

Spells or incantations for Fire, the South Quarter—

Energy from the South, fire, I call on you
Come into my circle and
Assist me in my magic.
Your power is strong,
Your force is cleansing.
Protect me from uninvited forces
As I do my work
Help keep my intentions pure,
Shore up my resolve,

Hear me now, hear my call.
Blessed be

Spells or incantations for Air, the East Quarter—

I call to you here and now
Oh great element of air.
With intent my forces blend
With your swirling forces
Working together to the end.
Open my mind and
Whisper the secrets I need to help me
Harming none and blessing all,
Hear me now, heed my call.
Blessed be

Spells or incantations for water, the West Quarter:

I call to you here and now
Oh great element of water.
With intent my forces blend
With your ever-flowing forces
To wash over me and
Give me the wisdom to
Open my mind to accomplish my magic
Working together to the end.
Harming none and blessing all,

Hear me now, heed my call.
Blessed be

From Talismans, Amulets, Lucky Charms & Symbols

Hail all mighty powers of the universe
Bring light, love, and energy into my stone
That it might forevermore protect
And guide me.
So mote it be

All powers of the universe
Assist me now as I cleanse
Charge
And consecrate
This symbol
Keep my focus clear
And my intention pure
Make my energy one with yours
As we power this symbol
So mote it be

From Poppets, Voodoo Dolls and Effigies

While using a Poppet for healing

I've created you in ____________________ image
You are ____________________ and they are you.
As this candle burns, good health returns.

Voodoo Doll Binding

I bind it left,
I bind it right,
No more music,
Now or tonight.

Effigy Banishing

Burn baby, burn.

I banish you from my life
Never shall you return
I'm free of you, You're free of me
This is how it shall always be.

From Familiars, Thought Forms, and Energy Balls

Familiar

By the morning sun that shines,
And the moon that glows at night,
I summon you to bring to me
A Familiar who is right.
A bark, a tweet, a croak, a mew,
That I may know it's true.
Hear me now, hear my plea,
And join me with
The one who's meant to be.
Blessed be.

Thoughtform

I send this Thoughtform on its way,
To do my bidding, now, today.
Bring success for my business,
Bring it fast I say.
Go, now, be on your way!

Energy Ball

I send the yellow ball
Along the way.
To protect my ____________
Come what may.
Go now, do your thing

Take care of my loved one
Today.

Reminder

PLEASE remember, there is no right or wrong way to perform your rituals and spells. Magic is personal and what works for some may not work for others. By all means attempt the tried and true methods but don't be afraid to add your own personal touch to your craft. If something feels right, it is usually right. By the same token if something feels wrong, it is usually wrong.

I am happy to share what works for me and if it works for you, so much the better. The keywords to remember are **concentration, regularity, intent, focus,** and **purpose.** Solitary and eclectic witches will perform their magic differently than covens. It is still magic.

Finally

If you are new to the craft, just beginning your journey, try to use very basic techniques so you don't become frustrated if things don't turn out the way you want them to.

Different magic practitioners, witches, or witchcraft traditions will practice using the elements differently. If you are a part of a certain coven, group, circle, gathering, or tradition, you should look into the practice they use and follow through with that tradition.

Permission, understanding, and intent are key words when using magic. Intent is powerful because if your intent is not strong, your magic will not be strong. Your intent must be spot on for magic to work. I believe most people who dabble in magic fully understand the outcomes and consequences.

When repeating incantations in your circle or at your altar, repeat them as often as necessary until you ***feel*** your energy and power changing and growing.

By all means, practice, practice, practice! And, log your journey. When you find your niche, you will know you are home.

Finally, when you become adept at working with Magic entities, you may find you have a favorite. Mine is Thought Forms!

Coming soon from E.M. Fairchilde

Cleansing, Charging & Consecrating

Printed in Great Britain
by Amazon

47934286R00078